Contents

KT-210-203

General techniques

A knot pattern is given with the instructions of each piece of jewellery. Before starting, look to see which knots you will have to tie and read the instructions on how to tie them (see page 5).

Bracelet technique

For the bracelets that are included with the necklaces, follow the instructions given for *Necklace technique*. Therefore, first tie a Basic Knot, then add a bead and then follow the knot pattern. The bracelets with Whole Macramé Knots are finished as follows: Measure the wrist and add an extra 6 cm. Note: it must be possible to slide the bracelet over your hand. Start tying the bracelet according to the knot pattern for the necklace. Once you have tied a couple of knots, place the ends of the Scoubidou strands you are not tying with over each other. Use adhesive tape to stick the strands together to make a kind of circle. Next, continue tying knots according to the pattern, only now tie them over 2 strands. Do this all the way around the circle. It does not matter if the knots do not touch each other if the Scoubidou strand is finished.

Necklace technique

Find the middle of the Scoubidou strand and tie a Basic Knot. Do not pull it too tight, because this knot will be untied later. Thread the middle bead onto the strand and tie the knot, which is given in the knot pattern for the necklace. Do this on one side first (right) and then the other (left). This way, you will be able to see exactly how much of the Scoubidou strand you will use on the left and right. There will sometimes be a bit of Scoubidou strand left over on one side or the other where you tie the knots.

Starting

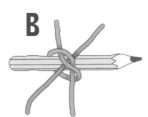

Diagram A shows you how to start when making a key ring. If you have to start with a loop, it is useful to use a pencil to help you (B). *General techniques* gives a description of how to fasten a necklace.

Finishing

There are different ways of tying the ends of the strands:
- Tie a regular knot and pull it tight.
- Add a bead to the end. Tie a small knot after the bead and apply a small amount of jewellery glue between the bead and the knot.
- Use a large needle with a large eye to thread the Scoubidou strands to the back of the piece of jewellery.
- With a jewellery catch. Use a pair of flat-nose pliers to pinch the Scoubidou strand between the catch. It is not easy to use a pair of pliers. Ask an adult for some help if you cannot do it.
- With a Basic Round Knot which ends in the middle (see the diagram of the Basic Round Knot at the end of page 9).

SCOUBIDOU JEWELLERY

Corien van Tienhoven

SEARCH PRESS

Preface

This edition published
in 2005 by Search
Press Ltd, Wellwood,
North Farm Road,
Tunbridge Wells,
Kent, TN2 3DR

First published in
The Netherlands
2004 by
Forte Publishers,
Utrecht.
Original title:
Scoebidoe sieraden.
© Forte Uitgevers BV,
P.O. Box 1394,
3511 BJ Utrecht,
The Netherlands.

Editor: Irene de Vette
Illustrations: Jill van der Pas
Photography and digital image editing:
Fotografie Gerhard Witteveen,
Apeldoorn, the Netherlands
Design and translation: Textcase,
Hilversum, the Netherlands
Cover design: Bade creatieve communicatie BV,
Baarn, the Netherlands

During a holiday in France, I discovered Scoubidou when I saw bunches of brightly coloured strands hanging in markets everywhere. There are so many different things you can do with Scoubidou strands. Not only can you use them to make key rings, but also attractive jewellery. Scoubidou strands can be purchased in most toy shops and craft shops.
I started to use them immediately with another summer fad in the back of my mind: jewellery making.
There is a big difference in the quality of the strands. The cheaper strands do not tie so well when making jewellery and they break more easily.
You can combine many different materials with Scoubidou strands, for example beads, clay and buttons. Check your craft box, maybe you will find other materials, which you can use.
Have fun with the examples given in this book and with inventing other Scoubidou ideas!

Corien van Tienhoven

All rights reserved. No part of this book, text, photographs or
illustrations may be reproduced or transmitted in any form or by any means
by print, photoprint,microfilm, microfiche, photocopier, internet or in any way
known or as yet unknown, or stored in a retrieval system, without written
permission obtained beforehand from Search Press.

Reprinted 2005

ISBN 1 84448 120 4

The publishers and author can accept no responsibility for any consequences
arising from the infomation, advice, or instructions given in this publication.
Readers are permitted to reproduce any of the items in this book for
their personal use, or for the purposes of selling for charity, free of charge and
without the prior permission of the Publishers. Any use of the items for commercial
purposes is not permitted without the prior permission of the Publishers.

UK Sole Importer of The Original Scoubidou Strands:
Purple Rhino Scoubidou
website: www.scoubidou.uk.com / email: sales@scoubidou.uk.com

How to tie knots

Semi Macramé Knot

The pink strand and the green strand are the knotting Scoubidou strands. The knot is made by tying these 2 Scoubidou strands around the blue strands. You can also make the knot slightly thinner by tying the strand around only one blue strand.

- Step 1: Place the green Scoubidou strand over the 2 blue strands (A).

  - Step 2: Place the pink strand over the green strand (A).

A

- Step 3: Thread the pink strand from left to right under the blue strand (B).

B

- Step 4: Thread the pink Scoubidou strand from the back to the front between the blue strand and the green strand (C).

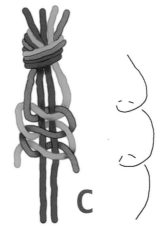

C

These 4 steps will give you a Semi Macramé Knot. If you start each time with the Scoubidou strand farthest to the right, i.e. you keep repeating the Semi Macramé Knot, the knot will start to turn (D).

D

Whole Macramé Knot

If you continue from step 4, then you will get a Whole Macramé Knot.

- Step 5: Place the green over the blue strand (E).

- Step 6: Place the pink strand over the green strand (E).

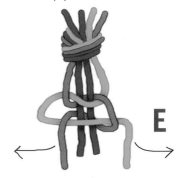

E

- Step 7: Thread the pink Scoubidou strand from right to left under the blue Scoubidou strands.

- Step 8: Thread the pink strand from the back to the front between the blue and the green strand (F).

F

You will now have a Whole Macramé Knot. If you repeat these 8 steps, the knots will stay flat.

How to tie knots

Lark's Head Knot

You can tie the Lark's Head Knot around one strand. You can also tie it around 2 or more strands if you wish to make the necklace thicker.

- Step 1: Thread the red strand
from right
to left
under
the blue
strand
(A).

- Step 2:
Thread the red strand from left to right over the blue one and from front to back between the blue and the red one (B).

By repeating steps 1 and 2, the knot will start turning (C).

You can also make the Lark's Head Knot straight.

- Step 1: Thread the red Scoubidou strand under the blue strand.

- Step 2: Thread the red strand back over the blue Scoubidou strand and then between the red strand and the blue strand on the left-hand side.

- Step 3: Thread the red Scoubidou strand over the blue Scoubidou strand.

- Step 4: Thread the red Scoubidou strand under the blue strand and over the red Scoubidou strand.

In this way the knot will remain straight

Front straight Lark's Head Knot

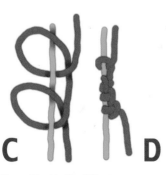

Turned Lark's Head Knot

Back straight Lark's Head Knot

Basic Straight Knot

You need either 4 Scoubidou strands or 2 strands folded double to tie a straight Basic Straight Knot. The method used is given for each piece of jewellery. If you tie this knot correctly, you will always have a square. This is a good way of checking whether the knot has been tied correctly or not.

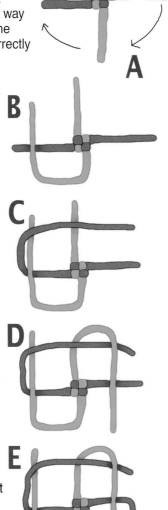

A

Basic Straight Knot right-hand side

B

- Step 1: Place the bottom pink strand over the right-hand green Scoubidou strand and leave it hanging (B).

C

- Step 2: Place the right-hand green Scoubidou strand over the top pink strand and leave it hanging (C).

D

- Step 3: Place the top pink strand over the left-hand green Scoubidou strand and leave it hanging (D).

E

- Step 4: Thread the left-hand green strand from the front to the back through the pink loop, which you have made (E).

The knot will look like a flower. Carefully pull all 4 Scoubidou strands. Once you are sure that the knot has been tied correctly, you can then pull the strands tight. The knot described has been tied to the right. If you tie another knot to the right, your Scoubidou jewellery will start to turn. If you tie the next knot to the left, then the Basic Straight Knot will remain straight.

Basic Straight Knot left-hand side

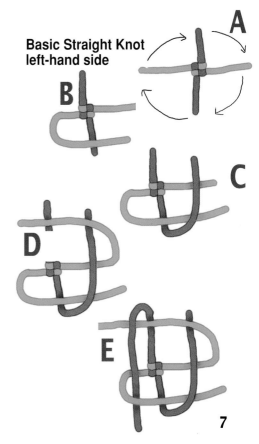

A

B

C

D

E

7

How to tie knots

Basic Knot with 3 Strands

- Step 1: Place the green Scoubidou strand over the blue Scoubidou strand and leave it hanging.

- Step 2: Place the blue Scoubidou strand over the pink Scoubidou strand and leave it hanging.

- Step 3: Push the pink Scoubidou strand from the front to the back through the green loop which you have made.

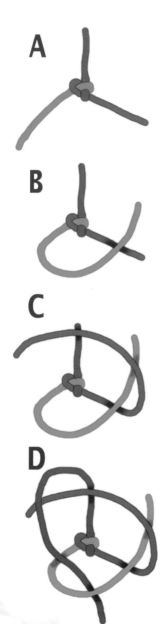

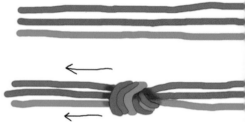

If you only tie the knots to the right, then the Scoubidou will start to turn. If you tie the knots alternately to the left and right, then the Scoubidou will remain straight.

To finish it, you can tie the Scoubidou so that the strands are in the middle and not on the side. You can do this by tying a Basic Round Knot.

Basic Round Knot

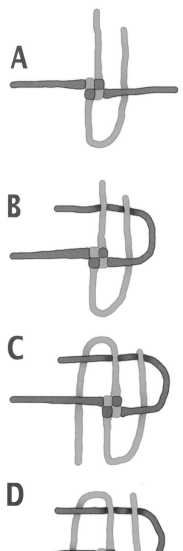

- Step 1: Thread the bottom green Scoubidou strand under the right-hand pink strand (A).

- Step 2: Thread the right-hand pink Scoubidou strand under the top green strand (B).

- Step 3: Thread the top green strand under the left-hand pink Scoubidou strand (C).

- Step 4: Thread the left-hand pink Scoubidou strand from the back to the front through the green loop which you have made (D).

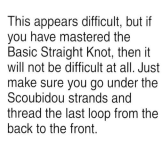

This appears difficult, but if you have mastered the Basic Straight Knot, then it will not be difficult at all. Just make sure you go under the Scoubidou strands and thread the last loop from the back to the front.

9

Flower Power

Materials
- 1 yellow Scoubidou strand
- 2 green Scoubidou strand
- 3 flower buttons

Bracelet

Method
1 strand is more than long enough to cut 2 pieces for a bracelet. Use two pieces yellow strand, each about 6 cm longer than the circumference of your wrist. Thread 1 flower button in the middle of the 2 yellow strands. Tie one Whole Macramé Knot about 2 cm below the flower button. Slide the knot up against the flower button (to create the leaves) then tie 3 Whole Macramé Knots, add 1 flower button and then tie 1 Whole Macramé Knot and slide it up.

Finish the bracelet as described in *Finishing*. You will not be able to tie the end Whole Macramé Knots so that they touch each other, because the strand is too short for that. You will have an 'empty' bit of strand where you will see the 2 core strands. The size of this gap depends on your wrist size.

A

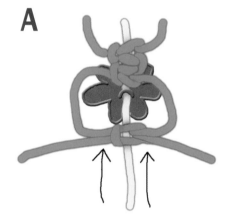

B

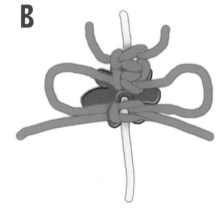

Materials
- Key ring
- 1 yellow Scoubidou strand
- 1 green Scoubidou strand
- 5 flower buttons

Key ring with yellow flowers

Method

Find the middle of the Scoubidou strand. Tie the green Scoubidou strand to the key ring with the yellow Scoubidou strand in the middle. The key ring jewellery is made using a Basic Straight Knot. Add a flower button every four knots. Tie the last flower button to the end.
Finish the Scoubidou. Use some scrap green Scoubidou strand to make the leaves. Fold them double and stick them between the flowers using a small amount of jewellery glue.

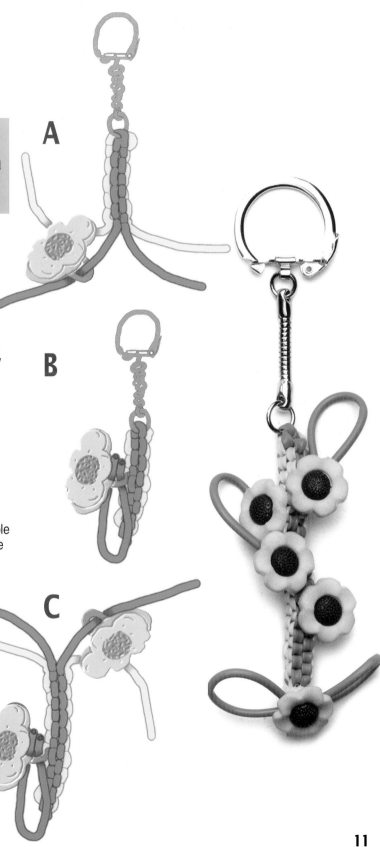

A

B

C

Materials
- 2 green Scoubidou strands
- 1 metal flower
- Key ring

Key ring with a metal flower

Method
Fold the Scoubidou strands double. Use a Lark's Head Knot to tie them to the flower. Tie Semi Macramé Knots until the knotting Scoubidou strands are almost finished (approximately 5 cm remaining). Cut the other core Scoubidou strand so that it is approximately 4 cm long. Fold this and use adhesive tape to stick it in place. Continue tying knots until the loop measures approximately 1 cm.
Finish the Scoubidou. Tie the loop to the key ring.

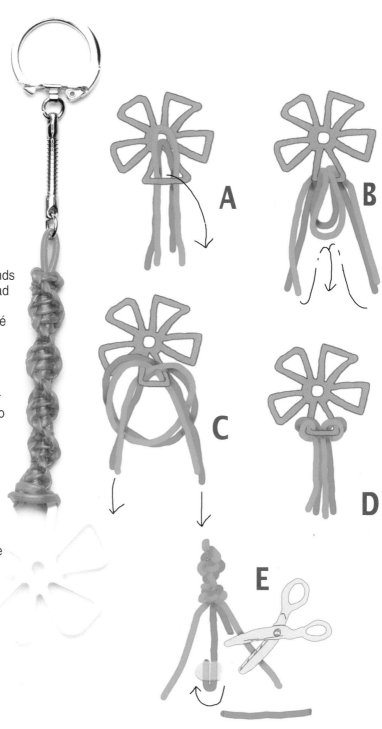

A

B

C

D

E

Cheerful jewellery

Necklace

Materials
- 2 wooden beads
- 1 large bead
- 2 red Scoubidou strands
- 2 yellow Scoubidou strands
- 1 jewellery catch
- Pair of flat-nosed pliers

Method
Right-hand knot pattern: thread on 1 large bead, tie 3 red Whole Macramé Knots, thread on 1 wooden bead, tie 6 yellow Whole Macramé Knots.

Left-hand knot pattern: tie 3 red Whole Macramé Knots, thread on 1 wooden bead, tie 6 yellow Whole Macramé Knots.
Finish the knotting strand. Cut the 2 core strands so that the necklace fits around your neck. Add a catch.

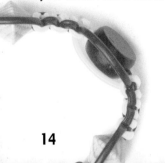

Earrings

Materials
- 2 earring hooks
- 2 metal rings
- 2 yellow beads
- 1 red Scoubidou strand
- 2 scrap yellow Scoubidou strands

Method

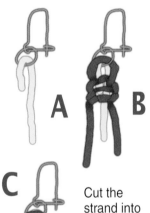

Cut the strand into 4 separate pieces. Fold the scrap piece of yellow strand over the ring (A). Then, fold a piece of red Scoubidou strand over the ring and tie 10 Semi Macramé Knots (B). First over 2 strands and then over 1 Scoubidou strand (C). Cut the 3 Scoubidou strands off. Insert the 3 Scoubidou strands into the bead. Use a drop of glue to keep the bead in place.

Bracelet

Materials
- 3 wooden beads
- 1 red Scoubidou strand
- 1 yellow Scoubidou strand
- 1 red and yellow Scoubidou strand cut to the size of your wrist + 6 cm

Method
Right-hand knot pattern: thread on 1 large bead, tie 3 yellow Whole Macramé Knots, thread on 1 wooden bead, tie 5 red Whole Macramé Knots.
Left-hand cutting pattern: tie 3 yellow Whole Macramé Knots, thread on 1 wooden bead, tie 5 large Whole Macramé Knots.
Finish the bracelet as described in *Finishing* (see page 4).

Summer jewellery

Necklace

Materials
- 2 yellow mother-of-pearl Scoubidou strands
- 2 orange mother-of-pearl Scoubidou strands
- 3 yellow beads
- 2 orange beads
- Jewellery catch and glue

Method
Right-hand knot pattern: thread a yellow bead onto 2 yellow Scoubidou strands, tie 2 orange Whole Macramé Knots, thread on 1 orange bead, tie 2 orange Whole Macramé Knots, thread 1 yellow bead onto the 2 yellow Scoubidou strands + 1 orange Scoubidou strand. Cut 1 orange Scoubidou strand so that it is 5 cm long. Apply a small amount of glue to the end of the orange Scoubidou strand and insert it into the orange bead. Tie another 6 yellow Whole Macramé Knots. Left-hand knot pattern: copy the right-hand knot pattern from the middle yellow bead. Finish the necklace with a catch (see *Finishing*, page 4).

Bracelet

Materials
- 2 yellow mother-of-pearl Scoubidou strands
- 1 orange mother-of-pearl Scoubidou strand
- 3 yellow beads
- Jewellery catch
- Jewellery glue

Method
Cut the orange Scoubidou strand in half. Right-hand knot pattern: thread a bead onto the 2 orange Scoubidou strands, tie 3 yellow Whole Macramé Knots and cut the orange Scoubidou strands so that they are about 3 cm long. Apply a small amount of glue to the ends of the orange strands and insert into the yellow bead. Finish with the catch.

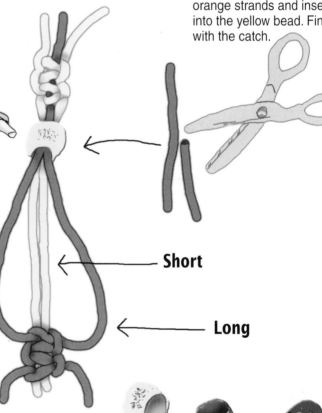

Short

Long

Beach set

Necklace

Materials
- 4 blue Scoubidou strands
- Orange and yellow Makin's Clay
- Makin's Clay sea mould
- Rings
- 2 jewellery beads
- Cocktail stick

Method
Start in the middle of the Scoubidou strands. Tie Semi Macramé Knots to the left and right until there is no more strand. Thread a jewellery bead onto both ends of the long blue Scoubidou strands and glue the ends of the knotting Scoubidou strands into the bead (A + B). Use Makin's Clay to make some shells.

Bracelet

Materials
- 2 blue Scoubidou strands
- 2 pieces of blue Scoubidou strand cut to the size of your wrist
- 1 jewellery bead
- Shells

Method
Start in the middle of the strands. Tie Semi Macramé Knots to the left and right until there is no more strand. Close it by gluing the ends into a jewellery bead (A + B).

Earrings

Materials
- 2 earring hooks
- 2 rings
- 2 shells
- Pair of flat-nose pliers

Push a ring through the hole in the shell and use the flat-nose pliers to attach the ring to the earring hook.

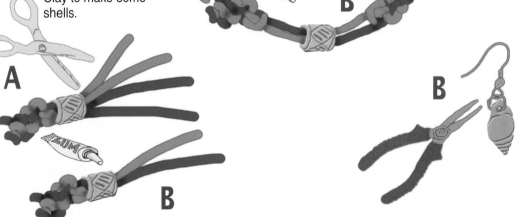

Make a rotating movement with a cocktail stick to make a small hole in the shells. Once the shells are dry (after approximately 24 hours), thread them onto a ring. Slide the rings onto a loop of the knot. Do not tie the necklace too tight, otherwise you will not be able to slide the rings onto the loops.

Materials
- 6 Scoubidou strands
- 6 glass beads
- 4 large jewellery beads
- 3 small jewellery beads

Method
Tie a knot in the 6 Scoubidou strands approximately 4 cm from the ends. Once the necklace is finished, you will add some beads to these 4 cm long pieces of strand. Divide the Scoubidou strands: 3 to each side (A + B + C). Left-hand knot pattern: Tie approximately 20 Semi

Macramé Knots with strand A + B. Tie them over one strand (C). Thread a large jewellery bead onto 3 Scoubidou strands. Tie strands C + B over strand A until there is almost nothing left of strand B. Thread the other jewellery bead onto strands C + A. Glue strand B into the jewellery bead. Cut strands A + C to the same length.

Tie the 3 Scoubidou strands on the right-hand side in the same way as the left-hand side.
Tie the left and right-hand A + C Scoubidou strands together to make a necklace.

For football fans

When making a bracelet, always start with the letter in the middle so that you know exactly how much you need.

Materials
- 1 red Scoubidou strand
- 1 black Scoubidou strand
- 1 white Scoubidou strand
- Letter beads
- Black Identi-pen
- Red, black and white melting beads
- Key ring
- White, red and black beads

4 Scoubidou strands fit through the hole in the square letter beads. 2 Scoubidou strands fit through the hole in the melting beads.

Method key ring

'Ajax'
Fold 1 white Scoubidou strand double over the ring of the key ring. Thread 1 red melting bead onto the 2 white strands.
Knot pattern: thread on letter "A", insert 1 red + 1 black strand into the letter "A" and use jewellery glue to stick them in place, tie 3 Semi Macramé Knots, thread letter "J" on 4 strands, etc. To finish it,

thread 2 strands through 1 melting bead and cut off the ends.

'Feyenoord'

Fold 1 white strand over the ring of the key ring.
Knot pattern: thread 1 red square bead with a heart onto 2 white strands, insert 1 red + 1 black strand into the square bead using jewellery glue to hold them in place, tie 1 red Whole Macramé Knot, thread letter "F" onto 2 white strands, tie 1 black Whole Macramé Knot, thread on letter "E", etc. To finish it, tie the ends in a knot.

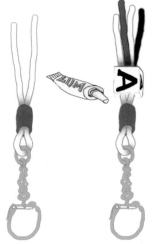

Method bracelet

Start in the middle of the strand. Thread 1 white melting bead onto 1 white middle strand, thread 1 melting bead onto both knotting strands, tie 1 black Whole Macramé Knot, thread on the next white bead, etc. Finish as described in *Bracelet technique* (see page 4).

'PSV'

Use the Basic Knot with 3 Strands tied to the right. Knot pattern: tie a knot in the 3 Scoubidou strands, tie

5 Basic Straight Knots, thread 1 melting bead on each strand, tie 5 knots, thread the letter "P" on 3 Scoubidou strands, tie 2 knots, thread on the letter "S", tie 2 knots, thread on the letter "V", tie 5 knots. Finish by tying 1 large knot in the Scoubidou strands.

Of course, you can change the colours and letters to match your favourite football team.

Necklace

Materials
- 2 orange Scoubidou strands
- 5 (different) jewellery beads
- Jewellery glue

Method
Left-hand knot pattern: thread a jewellery bead onto 2 Scoubidou strands, tie 4 Lark's Head Knots, thread on 1 jewellery bead, tie 4 Lark's Head Knots. Finishing: glue the strand into the jewellery bead. Right-hand knot pattern, from the jewellery bead: tie 4 Lark's Head Knots, thread on 1 jewellery bead, tie 4 Lark's Head Knots and finish.

Bracelet

Materials
- 1 orange Scoubidou strand
- 1 orange Scoubidou strand cut to the size of your wrist
- 3 jewellery beads
- Jewellery catch

Method
Left-hand knot pattern: thread the jewellery bead onto the 2 Scoubidou strands, tie turned Lark's Head Knots until the strand is finished.

Finishing: glue the strand inside the jewellery bead. Right-hand knot pattern, from the jewellery bead: tie turned Lark's Head Knots until the strand is finished. Finishing: glue the strand into the jewellery bead. Note: it will look the best if the left and right-hand sides are the same length. Finish the bracelet with a jewellery catch.

Neon jewellery

Necklace

Materials

- 2 pink Scoubidou strands
- 2 green Scoubidou strands
- 27 yellow melting beads
- 27 pink melting beads
- Hexagonal bead template
- Jewellery glue
- Metal rings

Method

Left-hand knot pattern: tie a regular knot in the middle of the 4 Scoubidou strands, tie 1 pink Whole Macramé Knot, thread 1 bead onto each tying strand, tie 1 green Whole Macramé Knot, thread on some beads, tie 1 pink Whole Macramé Knot, etc.
Tie 10 Whole Macramé Knots. Thread a bead onto 1 middle strand and glue the ends of the strand inside the bead. Do this with the other middle strand as well.
Right-hand knot pattern: after the regular knot, start with a green Whole Macramé Knot and then follow the left-hand knot pattern.
Finishing: you can finish it by tying a regular knot when you put it on or by adding a jewellery catch.

For the pendant

Place a flower pattern on the hexagonal bead template. Make 5 flowers, or more if you also make the bracelet.
Melt the beads together. Thread the ring onto the pendant and slide it onto the regular knot you made. Glue 2 beads to the back of the small flowers. Leave them to dry properly.

Neon jewellery

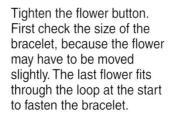

Bracelet

Materials
- 1 yellow Scoubidou strand
- 2 green Scoubidou strands
- 27 pink melting beads
- 20 yellow melting beads
- Glue
- 1 yellow flower button

Method
Fold the yellow strand double. Tie a knot around a pencil (see *Finishing*, page 4). The flower button must fit through the loop which is made using the pencil. This button is used to fasten the bracelet.

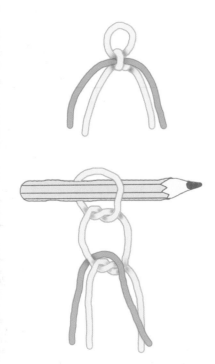

Tighten the flower button. First check the size of the bracelet, because the flower may have to be moved slightly. The last flower fits through the loop at the start to fasten the bracelet.

Earrings

Materials
- 2 scrap pink Scoubidou strands
- 2 green melting beads
- 2 yellow melting beads
- 2 earring hooks
- 2 medium-sized metal rings
- Jewellery glue

Method
Cut the pink Scoubidou strand to the size you wish to have the earrings. Thread the yellow melting bead onto the pink Scoubidou strand (A). Bend the ring open. Thread the green bead onto the ring (B). Apply a small amount of glue into the green bead (C). Push the ends of the scrap pink Scoubidou strand into the green bead and hold them in place. Only let go once the glue has dried.

A

B

C

Necklace
(see page 1 for a picture
of this necklace)

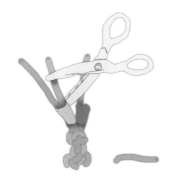

Materials
- 2 pink Scoubidou strands
- 2 lilac Scoubidou strands
- 1 metal flower (eyelet tag)
- 6 lilac melting beads
- 6 pink melting beads
- Jewellery glue

Method for the left and right-hand sides
Find the middle of a pink
strand and a lilac strand.
Use a Lark's Head Knot to

Finishing: the necklace can
be tied with a regular knot
when you put it on or you
can add a jewellery catch.

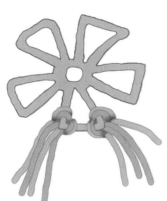

tie them to the flower. Tie
20 Semi Macramé Knots,
thread on 2 pink beads and
2 lilac beads, tie 10 Semi
Macramé Knots. Thread the
2 beads onto the middle
strands. Glue the ends of
the strands into the bead.
If necessary, tie a few more
knots in the strands.

Key ring with bells

Materials
- 1 pink Scoubidou strand
- 1 lilac Scoubidou strand
- Metal rings
- Bells
- Key ring

Method
Tie the Scoubidou strands to the key ring (see *Finishing*, page 4). Tie Basic Round Knots until there is no more strand left. Tie a regular knot in the end or finish the ends with a Basic Straight Knot where the Scoubidou strands end in the middle. Thread the bells onto the rings and tie the rings to the loops.

Bracelet with letters

Materials
- 1 pink Scoubidou strand
- 1 lilac Scoubidou strand
- 1 green Scoubidou strand
- Coloured letter beads

Method
Left and right-hand knot patterns: start in the centre with a letter (the middle letter of the name), tie a couple of Basic Round Knots, add a letter, etc. You can use 3 or 4 Scoubidou strands. Finish with a regular knot.

Playing with scraps

Materials
- 2 red Scoubidou strands
- Scrap Scoubidou strands of different colours
- Beads
- Nylon thread
- Pair of pliers
- Metal rings
- Wire (Ø 0.5 mm)
- Pair of round-nose pliers
- Makin's Clay
- Cookie cutters (heart)

Necklace
Thread beads and pieces of strand alternately onto the nylon thread. Use a large Makin's Clay heart as a pendant.

Bracelet
Use a pair of pliers to cut a piece of wire to the same size as your wrist. Use a pair of round-nose pliers to make a loop at one end. Thread the pieces of strand and the hearts onto the wire. Bend the last piece of wire into a hook.

Method
Cut the scrap Scoubidou strands into small pieces. Make the hearts from Makin's Clay. Use a cocktail stick to make a hole in the shapes.

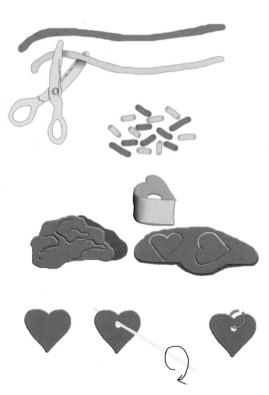